Toward A Hope-Filled Life

A Bible Study

John W. Clarke

CSS Publishing Company, Inc., Lima, Ohio

TOWARD A HOPE-FILLED LIFE

Library of Congress Cataloging-in-Publication Data

Clarke, John William, 1967-
Toward a hope-filled life : a Bible study / John W. Clarke.
p. cm.
ISBN 0-7880-2569-4 (perfect bound : alk. paper)
1. Hope—Biblical teaching. 2. Hope—Religious aspects—Christianity. I. Title.

BS680.H7C53 2008
234'.25—dc22

2007044613

For more information about CSS Publishing Company resources, visit our website at www.csspub.com or email us at csr@csspub.com or call (800) 241-4056.

Cover design by Barbara Spencer
ISBN-13: 978-0-7880-2569-3
ISBN-10: 0-7880-2569-4

PRINTED IN USA

To my son
John Wayne Clarke Jr.
for continually moving
toward a hope-filled life

So I pray that God, who gives you hope, will keep you happy and full of peace as you believe in him. May you overflow with hope through the power of the Holy Spirit.
— Romans 15:13

Table Of Contents

Introduction

Hope: Where Does It Come From — How Can You Get Some?

In his autobiography, *Breaking Barriers*, syndicated columnist, Carl Rowan, tells about a teacher who greatly influenced his life. Rowan relates: Miss Thompson reached into her desk drawer and pulled out a piece of paper containing a quote attributed to Chicago architect, Daniel Burnham. I listened intently as she read, "Make no little plans; they have no magic to stir men's blood and probably themselves will not be realized. Make big plans, aim high in hope and work. Remember that our sons and grandsons are going to do things that would stagger us."

More than thirty years ago, I gave a speech in which I said that Miss Frances Thompson had given me a desperately needed belief in myself. A newspaper printed the story, and someone mailed the clipping to my beloved teacher. She wrote me: "You have no idea what that newspaper story meant to me. For years, I have endured my brother's arguments that I had wasted my life — that I should have married and had a family. When I read that you gave me credit for helping to launch a marvelous career, I put the clipping in front of my brother. After he read it, I said, 'You see, I didn't really waste my life, did I?' " Encouragement and praise is like a boomerang: The more you give it, the more it wants to return. It's really just a matter of knowing this that can make all the difference not only in your life but in the lives of those around you. Not that we live for praise ourselves. Rather, the more satisfaction we have in giving merely serves to fuel our desire to keep it coming. Find someone today who needs your encouragement, a little appreciation. Let your praise fly and then step back. You'll want to be ready to catch it on the rebound.[1]

Hope is like that. You'll want to be ready to catch it on the rebound. When hope is lost, a piece of life is cut loose and the person who finds himself without hope, finds himself in a position of vulnerability. We are not strong when we are feeling inadequate to the demands of the world around us. The apostle Paul knew this and wrote in Romans 8:25: "For in hope we are saved. Now hope that is seen is not hope. For who hopes for what is seen? But if we hope for what we do not see, we wait for it with patience." Imagine waking each day and not being able to look forward to something. The something I speak of is what cannot be seen, but can be hoped for. David Lloyd George wrote, "Hope is a commitment, not a hilarious celebration. No army can march on a retreating mind. And so hope is sewn into the very fabric of who we are and nurturing that hope will allow us to become the children of God that we are designed to be."

Hope is something that we are born with, it is within us, but hope does not peek out at the world unless we feed it and allow it to grow. Hope is an option. We may not be fully in control of all the many things that can happen to us in the living of life. We may not be able to stop certain things from happening to us.

There are certain illnesses that simply make themselves manifest without any warning. They can, and often do, destroy a person's sense of well-being. The fact remains that hope is a response that can lead us through whatever problems life throws our way. The problem may well win out, but that does not mean that we are without a sense of possibility even in the midst of tragedy. As a local church pastor, I see hope in the midst of suffering all the time. It would be difficult to recount the number of times that I have walked into the room of a sick parishioner and left renewed and filled with hope. I had gone into the room to offer the presence of Christ to that person. My visit was to help lift the burden of whatever illness the person was suffering from. My prayer was intended to help in the healing of that child of God. And, in most cases, that prayer was delivered and the person who was the object of that prayer benefited from it in some way.

But, usually by the time I was ready to leave the room, the person who was ill became the person of hope. Through the prism of whatever illness they were dealing with, they were able to show forth a visible picture of hope. That picture usually resided in the way they looked or spoke, or both. That is not to say that sometimes people are so ill they cannot hear or respond. Sometimes the person will not recover from whatever their illness. But, then, and most especially then, the hope they had experienced through their understanding of the resurrection had already set in and allowed them to slip into death's rebirth without fear.

A Christian should be a person who understands the difference between a life well lived or a life just lived. From the time we are born we are destined to die! Saying that always puts a damper on things, but it is true. It is important how the life we have been blessed with is lived. Will we live it hopefully, or will we live it by the numbers, making sure not to take many chances and securing and insuring our lives are lived by the rules? We have been programmed to believe that if we live by the rules, things will go well. Conversely, if we live outside the lines, we are taught that it is likely we will crash and burn. People of hope live outside the lines! We can play the game of life and look like we are in control and look like we are the better for it. But, by being children of hope, children of a loving God, we live lives that reflect new possibilities at every important moment of life. People of hope always put the pedal to the metal. People of hope understand that it is okay to let go.

The fact is that Christians understand that God has already intervened in our lives and showed us a better way. God has showed us, through Jesus, that living in hope means not living in fear. Living as people of hope means that we look the evil of life square in the eye and show by example that we are not going to be captured by fear, because we have been freed by hope. First John 4:18, says, "There is no fear in love, but perfect love casts out fear." Being people of hope by definition means that we are free to make fun of the downs of life because we can enjoy the ups so much more than those who have no hope.

It is my prayer that the pages that follow will serve as a catalyst in moving you toward a hope-filled life. God has designed us to live life as a gift. We will all be better prepared to share that gift with the rest of the world if we incorporate into our lives a sense of hope for tomorrow. I hope you will be moved to engage in thinking about the great sacrifice that has been given so that we may be people of hope. We are offered the engine of life as it has been given to us in Jesus Christ. That engine is eternal and cannot be defeated. It is the engine, the energy, that we call hope!

---

1. Carl Rowan, "Breaking Barriers" in *Reader's Digest*, January 1992, Little Brown.

Chapter One

Let's Get Down To Basics

Hope has the potential of making all of us stronger and better focused. It allows us to endure the up and down motion of life by nudging us to look into the future. Hope allows us to vault over the problems of the moment, thus reducing those problems into more manageable issues that cannot defeat us. Hope gives us new vision, what a Christian may call "resurrection vision." That is the vision that encourages us to reduce the problems and inflate the possibilities because, after all, hope is quite literally, eternal.

As Christians, we are always encouraged to wait on the working of the Holy Spirit. No discussion of hope would be complete without the inclusion of the importance of the Holy Spirit. When incorporated into one's life, the Holy Spirit is almost like having your own travel agent. Any good travel agent will help you maneuver around the obstacles that may hinder your journey. When the Christian surrenders himself to the working of the Holy Spirit, that person then finds himself enabled and empowered to move ahead without fear of getting lost. It is sort of like having your best friend travel with you. There is always a sense of strength in numbers. No one likes to go on any trip alone. It is reassuring to have someone with you, someone you truly can trust with your life.

Most of us have seen a formation of geese flying overhead. They seem to be effortlessly gliding through space. Yet, these birds fly in a very special formation. The formation allows them to travel in the most efficient manner possible. As each goose flaps its wings it creates, much like an airplane, an uplift that both propels them forward while simultaneously creating an uplift for those behind. By flying in formation the way they do, they are able to fly much further than any one bird could fly alone.

If one of the geese cannot keep up with the formation and falls behind, it will suddenly feel the weight of not having the uplift from the birds in front. Because of this, barring some other reason, it will quickly move itself back into formation and take advantage of the lifting power of the bird in front of it.

The Holy Spirit is much like that flock of geese. The Holy Spirit lifts us and moves us along. It is especially important if we fall behind the others who are traveling with us. The moral to that story is simple. We should have as much sense as a goose and stay in formation so that we can discover where it is we are going and have the strength to reach our destination.

As we already know, that formation of geese has a leader. The leader will tire more quickly than the others because the leader is taking the world head on. When the leader feels tired, it rotates back into the formation and one of the other geese moves up to take its place. Our lesson from the geese is that it is important to take turns doing the difficult tasks and sharing those tasks with others. In this instance, we are speaking of relying on the Holy Spirit to step in and help when we are tired from being the one out front all the time. It is important that we find hope in being interdependent on each other. It is not a weakness to seek help, it is a strength.

Geese flying in formation honk to encourage those up front to keep up their speed. We have all heard them flying overhead, honking away. The Holy Spirit will push us to be an encouragement to those around us. The act of encouraging others will build us up and make us stronger for the journey.

When a goose gets sick, or shot down, two others from the formation will drop out of the group and follow the injured bird down to help protect it. They will stay with the injured bird until it gets well or dies. Then, they stretch their wings, run forward, and launch themselves into the air to catch up with the flock. If we have as much sense as geese, we will stand by each other in hard times as well as in good times. The gift of the Holy Spirit will help us to accomplish these things. There is hope in being a part of the flock!

No matter who we are or where we are from, we all live in the valley of the shadow of death. We do not wake up each day wondering if today is the day that we will die. Rather, we wake each day thinking that this day will be like other days, or it may even be a better day. We live hoping that the inevitable fact of death will be put off and we will be around to live another day. We are, by nature, a hopeful people. For those of us in the Christian community, our hope is one of the most basic expressions of our relationship to Jesus Christ. Jesus knew all about our hopes and our fears. He knew, because he, like us, lived with both.

People who have hope understand the difference between hope and wishing. The person of hope is the person who tests reality, the wisher looks toward some form of magical moment in which her or his wish will come to fruition. The following will serve as an example of someone who is a wisher, someone who really wants magic to happen. While hunting, Larry and Elmer got lost in the woods. Trying to reassure his friend, Larry said, "Don't worry. All we have to do is shoot into the air three times, stay where we are, and someone will find us." They shot in the air three times, but no one came. After a while, they tried again. Still no response. When they decided to try once more, Elmer said, "I hope it works this time. We're down to our last three arrows."

You see, Larry and Elmer were putting their hope in the advice of others, even though they didn't understand that the advice didn't apply to shooting arrows into the sky. People in difficult circumstances often rely on the advice of others. It is surprising how readily people will listen to a friend and put their trust in the advice of that friend, while ignoring God altogether. Larry and Elmer have placed their hope in the wisdom and experience of those they trust. That in itself is not a bad thing, unless that trust replaces the source of all hope in life, Jesus Christ. The book of Proverbs tells us, "Where there is no vision, the people perish" (Proverbs 29:18). That is, without hope, people huddle up in the corner and shoot arrows into the air. With no vision and no hope, the result is a life not fully lived. And in Hebrews we are told, "Because God wanted to make the unchanging nature of his purpose very clear to the heirs of what was promised, he confirmed it with an oath" (Hebrews 6:17).

What is promised is unchanging; it is unshakable. It is God's promise that we are going to inherit a hope that will allow us to fashion a way of life that is filled with eternal possibilities. We have this hope as the foundation upon which we find a secure footing in life. Finally, to complete this line of thought, we have the very familiar quote from Paul's letter to the church in Corinth, in which we are told that one of the three greatest gifts God gives us is "hope."

It is God's great pleasure to give us hope. But, hope does not mean that everything in life is going to be perfect. In fact, one of the gifts of hope is the ability to wait upon God and learn to trust in God, through that waiting, to be by our side through all the complexities that life offers. And why would God make us wait? Why would God delay in allowing us to live in the sunshine of hope fulfilled? One reason is so that we will gain an appreciation for what God gives when that hope does make an appearance in our life.

The person who understands hope, understands that she must defer to the transcendent power that has its own unfathomable purpose. The wisher, however, tries to bend and shape things in order to fit life as they live it. In short, the person who lives with hope allows God to be God. The person who is a wisher seeks to reverse some situation over which they no longer have control. The person who lives with hope can say along with Paul, "Now I see through a glass darkly...." The wisher wants to control the image seen in the mirror. There is a level of trust that the hope-filled person lives with. There is a measure of mistrust, fear, and loss of control that the wisher lives with.

One may also say that there is a third, but false, aspect of hope that should be looked at. The other side of hoping and even wishing is that of promising. What a person thinks God has promised will determine, to a large degree, how that person's character is shaped. Maybe a better way to explain the idea of promise is that the person who lives life thinking that God has promised her or him something, really needs to understand and be able to articulate exactly what they believe has been promised. In other words, what does God owe them? The person who lives with a sense of entitlement, a sense that God owes them some particular thing, is not likely to be a person who understands the concept of humility. They have not come to a point in life where they understand that God's promised presence is all that they will ever need.

As we attempt to define hope, we must begin and end with Jesus. Jesus believed that in God there was hope. Jesus believed so strongly in that hope that he was willing and did give his life on our behalf. Jesus' expression of faith in God is our reason to hope. That faith, that unshakable belief in God's love and in the life to come, led Paul and all of the early church leaders to spend their lives preaching the gospel and making it clear that they were willing to die for that gospel message. That is the ultimate expression of a hope-filled life!

Questions For Your Consideration

1. Who in your life has had an impact in the way you live out your faith?

2. What did Paul mean when he said hope that is seen is not hope?

3. What do you look forward to each day? What makes that "looking forward" important to your day-to-day living?

4. How does hope allow you to live outside the lines? What are those lines in your life?

5. The book of Proverbs tells us that "Where there is no vision, the people perish." What vision do you and your community of faith live by? How can you discover a new vision for the future?

6. What is a God-given hope?

7. Does living a hope-filled life mean you will be living a pain-free life? If not, why not?

8. Talk about your hope. Where does it come from and how can you pass it on to others?

9. In what way is Jesus the hope promised by God?

10. How can you nurture hope in your life today?

Chapter Two

Hope: How Is It Lived — How Is It Visible?

For most people, the real impact of hope becomes visible when life decides to throw us a set of circumstances that we have never encountered before. Most people do not think much about the future until some circumstance puts them into a thoughtful state of mind. We plan for the future by making sure our retirement funds are put aside. We dream of what it will be like to not have to work. But, we do not often think about the importance of confidence in the future until our present circumstances overload us with problems that seem more than we can bear. Most of us move through life in rather predictable ways. We are usually not aware of the power of problems until we run up against one so powerful that our daily life is no longer lived with its usual rhythm.

Most people are fortunate enough to live life without catastrophic problems. So we move through life oblivious to the need for hopeful foundations upon which to stand when the ground beneath us begins to shift. When that ground does begin to shift, and our lives also move in directions that put us off balance, we discover a need for a spiritual foundation upon which to stand. We find out that we need stability in our lives, even in the midst of those shifting sands. It is then that we reach out for something stronger than our own frail selves. We reach for something extra, but unless we have nurtured our life of hope, we are apt to discover that there is very little hope to support us when we need it most.

So, what should we do? We have all heard of people who overcome incredible odds in life. Usually, there are many twists and turns to the story of victory over obstacles that would seem insurmountable to most people. I would suggest, however, that the basic component to facing and overcoming the odds is hope. In fact, it is in choosing hope that success finds itself. A Christian person chooses to believe that the difference between life and death is a difference of hope; not magic, not a sense of entitlement, but hope based on the life, ministry, death, and resurrection of the one we call Savior, the carpenter from Nazareth, Jesus, who is Christ.

The word of God fills us with hope because it gives us examples of the faithfulness of God and the way God can and does work in our lives. There are many examples. Let's take a look at some of them. Consider the promise made to Abraham. He was told that he would be the father of many nations. God goes on to tell him that his wife, Sarah, is going to have a child. Abraham and Sarah are very old and certainly not in the position to conceive and raise a child. But, Genesis 21 tells us that God fulfills the promise made and Abraham and Sarah have a child. Hope, you see, is always on the table.

At the age of seventeen, Joseph received a vision that showed him that one day he would be a great man. Joseph was spoiled by his father. He was the apple of his father's eye. This fact did not exactly endear him to his brothers. As in many families, siblings can be cruel to one another. It was no different in Joseph's family. In fact, his brothers despised him and wanted to do him harm. They hated him to a degree that in today's world would send them to jail for the way they treated him. His brothers loathed him so much that they sold him into slavery. Later, when Joseph's vision became a reality and he was a powerful man in a position to change the lives of a nation, his brothers came to him seeking help. This time the brothers are the ones in need. Joseph, filled with hope, not hate, calmed their fears that he would seek revenge by saying to them that God has designs that we cannot even imagine. God used all of the bad circumstances of Joseph's life for good. Hope is once again fulfilled.

At a very tender age, David was given the promise that he would one day be a king. When he was introduced to Saul, and when he was perceived as a threat to Saul, he spent the next years of his life running from a man who now sought to kill him! But, in time, God peppered David with love and it is within that love that David felt hope where once he felt only despair.

Of course, we cannot forget the simple carpenter from Nazareth who became the king of the universe! We learn through stories like this that God's kind of hope comes to us through times of testing and times of encouragement. We learn about hope when we see ourselves in the biblical examples just mentioned, and many find hope in life when they become hope to someone else.

> *But he said to them, "The kings of the Gentiles lord it over them; and those in authority over them are called benefactors. But not so with you; rather the greatest among you must become like the youngest, and the leader like one who serves. For who is greater, the one who is at the table or the one who serves? Is it not the one at the table? But I am among you as one who serves."* — Luke 22:25-27

There is no better example of what it means to be a servant and how best to understand a servant's mindset than the prayer of Saint Francis.

> *God grant me the serenity*
> *to accept the things I cannot change,*
> *courage to change the things I can,*
> *and wisdom to know the difference.*

Sooner or later we all learn that the above prayer will influence how we live life. The nagging question is always the same question, "How can you really accept things you cannot change?" At what point in time do you finally understand that you do not have the answer to all of life's problems? It may be that there is something you can do. It may well be that you can temporarily help change something in someone's life that will help them. Human nature forces us to try and try again. It is not in our nature to simply stand back and say that some particular problem is just too big for us to grasp.

As a pastor, it is my good fortune to see the best of people. Many times, I have watched people in what appeared to be a hopeless situation rally and surprise everyone with the way in which they beat the odds. I have stood at the foot of the bed of many parishioners over the years and watched as hair fell out, as the ability to eat seemed lost, and as pain took hold of the person to the point of making everyone else feel the pain as if it were their own. But, through it all, the people never gave up on hope. Even when the end was near, they would smile with anticipation of that final hope, the hope eternal. Hope has a way of taking the sting out of the present by pulling us, sometimes reluctantly, into the future.

How that combination of present and future is lived out becomes visible in life as illustrated in the following story. This story comes from lecture notes I took in 1979 in a class dealing with how the church should respond to people with handicapping conditions. The professor was the Reverend Doctor Harold Wilke, a pioneer in encouraging the church to face the importance of ministry to people who live every day with a handicap.

> *I still think of Toby.*
>
> *What impressed me most about him was his mental attitude, a combination of calmness and serenity. Toby had been severely disabled from birth. He was now middle-aged. We used to meet two or three times a week. How often we heard him say, "So what?" When the local football team lost, he cocked his head to one side, smiled, and said, "So what?" That I did not find hard to understand. But I was amazed when his wheelchair had a flat tire and Toby just cocked his head, smiled, and said, "So what?" When something like this happened to me, I usually begin to shout. When the doctor told him he had only weeks left to live, Toby again said, "So what?" Even his mother could no longer understand him. "Aren't you carrying this too far, son?" she asked. But Toby said simply, "Listen, Mum! Is Easter only about eggs or also about me?"*
>
> *I thought that an absolutely wonderful remark though it made Toby seem somewhat strange to me. But later on, when his mother told me that her son, who had died on an Easter Sunday, had very seldom talked of his disability. Only once — they were having tea together and the boy — well, he was actually a grown-up — knocked a cup over and began to cry. A middle-aged man began to cry over a broken cup! Sobbing to himself, "I'm just an old cripple." Now when I think of Toby,*

he no longer seems strange to me. That business about Easter and the business of the cup — they go together. Toby had ideals, very high ideals. But he was human enough to know that our ideals cannot always be reached.

I shall still think of Toby — often.

— Ulrich Bach

There is a paradox in the idea of hope. On the one hand, hope signifies a confident expectation, a genuine trust, and a firm faith in God that reaches out beyond the tiny ideas we may harbor about what God will or will not do for humankind. It is the "So what?" of Toby. On the other hand, hope sometimes is the expression of wish, or a longing for something that we know deep inside our souls is not going to happen. Hope may, at times, seem like a link between reality and what we wish for in life. Hope is the promise of a second chance, another day; it is the possibility of the impossible. Hope makes the struggle worth our time and energy. It is in a very real sense a promise that God keeps with God's children.

Apart from faith, hope cannot exist. Some would argue that faith and hope should not be spoken of separately. Yet, hope is not to be confused with faith. Hope is not faith's twin; it is a separate member of the family. One of the major differences between faith and hope is that hope includes a yearning for something that is yet to come to completion and that something may in fact undergo a change in definition before hope is lived out and fulfilled. Life is simply not possible without hope. When a person has lost all hope, life ends. Without hope, there are no longer alternatives to life. It is the dropping of the teacup and the resulting comment, "I'm just an old cripple." Think about that — no alternatives — none! That is a harsh way to attempt the living of life.

Toby knew that every day was a new chance for hope to become a part of our lives. It is as if each new day is a vessel traveling the river of life. Christians should be able to come to a place of recognition where we confess that we cannot live life alone. There is freedom when we come to that understanding in our lives. Until we confess that we cannot do all of the things we know we should be doing in life on our own, or, just as importantly, those things we want to do and enjoy doing, we will never know what things may be accomplished.

When Hitler's reign of terror settled over France, hope seemed lost. Many people had to go underground, particularly those who represented the things dictators fear most — those things that communicated hope in the midst of despair. A quick look at history will tell you that there are few things feared more by tyrants than the arts. Creativity is a weapon of hope. In France, during the time they were occupied, many musicians and artists and others were forced to hide and were hunted by the feared Gestapo.

Choosing hope means not choosing fear. There is real freedom in choosing to not allow your God-given gifts to be taken away or to be used as tools against creativity! Choosing hope over fear means looking at every circumstance, even the loss of creativity, and proclaiming, "I can do all things through Christ who strengthens me" (Philippians 4:13).

In the town of Port Hope, Canada, there is a monument erected, not for the person who founded the town, not for some famous politician, but for a poor, unselfish, workingman who gave most of his time and energy to people who could never repay him. His name was Joseph Scriven, and he was born in Dublin in 1820. As a young man, he had the look of someone who was going to do something special in the world. He was engaged to the love of his life, but on the eve of their wedding, she accidentally fell in a pond and drowned. Joseph was understandably overcome with grief. Although he had graduated college and was on the brink of a promising career, he began to wander about, trying to forget his sorrow. His wanderings took him to Canada where he lived the remainder of his life. He became a devout Christian. He lived out his Christianity doing labor for people who could not pay and assisting the sick.

It was not until shortly before his death at age sixty that it was discovered he had a real gift for poetry. A friend, who was sitting with him while he was dying, discovered a poem Joseph had written to his mother in a time of deep sorrow; not intending that anyone else would see it. His poem was later set to music and has become a hymn known throughout Christendom. In polls taken to determine the popularity of hymns and gospel songs, his poem always appears near the top. What was his poem?

What a friend we have in Jesus.
All our sins and griefs to bear.
What a privilege to carry,
Everything to God in prayer.
Oh, what peace we often forfeit,
Oh, what needless pain we bear;
All because we do not carry,
Everything to God in prayer.

Joseph Scriven found freedom in hope by using the gifts he had been blessed with to make life better for others. Hope finds its way into life because God has equipped us with a unique ability to lift the load of those who are burdened. Our hope is summarized by Paul in his letter to the church in Rome, "May the God of hope fill you with all joy and peace as you trust in him, so that you may overflow with hope by the power of the Holy Spirit" (Romans 15:13).

Jacques Ellul, a French theologian, says this about Christian hope.

> *It must be remembered, of course, that Christian hope is more than a vague hope that things will be better tomorrow, or a stupid obstinacy that it will work out successfully next time, or confidence in human nature that it will survive the next test, too, after getting through so many, or the assurance that is based on a philosophy of history. Christian hope is none of these things. It does not rest on man or on objective mechanisms. It is a response of man to God's work for him.*[1]

For some people, hope may simply be the expression of a vain wish, a futile longing, a pathetic yearning for that which can never be, but which appears so enticing and so desirable that its possibility cannot be lightly dismissed. Hope may also be seen as the link between reality and desire, between sorrow and joy, or between suffering and release. It is the promise of tomorrow that makes today endurable; it is the possibility of victory that makes the struggle worthwhile; it is the assurance of life that transcends the agony of death. But, apart from faith, hope cannot exist at all. Yet, hope is not a synonym for faith. Hope is not the same as faith. It includes something that faith does not. It includes a dream for things that have yet to find completion in life and that may, over time, undergo change that transforms even what we had initially hoped for.

In other words, God acts, we react. God demonstrated eternal love through Jesus, and it is that love that overturns all of our preconceived notions of the limitations of life as we know it. It is in response to that self-giving and life-giving love that we are allowed to live life on a totally different and hope-filled path. We are allowed to live on a path that is defined by a positive expectation, filled with trust and patience, because we recognize that, apart from hope, no life is possible.

---

1. Jacques Ellul, *The Ethics of Freedom* (Grand Rapids, Michigan: Wm. B. Eerdmans, 1976), p. 12.

Questions For Your Consideration

1. How have you found hope in what appeared to be hopeless situations?

2. Give a biblical example from your own experience that shows forth a biblical influence of hope in your life.

3. How do the circumstances of Joseph's life impact your sense of what it means to be our sister's or brother's keeper?

4. The prayer of Saint Francis asks us to accept the things we cannot change. How do you accept what you cannot change and find room for hope in the midst of that fact of life?

5. What things in your life are there that you can say along with Toby, "So what?" These would be things that may seem difficult to others. Why?

6. In what way is creativity hopeful for you? How do you express that part of you that is creative?

7. What are the things that rob you of your ability to be creative? How do you rid yourself of those things?

8. Turn to Philippians 4:13. How can you do all things through Christ? What does that mean?

9. What hope-filled things do you do to help another feel hope in life?

10. What is the difference between hope and faith? In what ways are they the same?

Chapter Three

Hope: An Expectation Of Something Yet To Be

Hope, as it has been pointed out, is in many ways the expectation that there is something yet to happen in our lives or the lives of those we love. Hope implies a sense of anticipation, a feeling that we do not have everything in life figured out just yet. It is that kind of feeling of expectation that allows us to feel a sense of courage in the presence of doubt and despair. The thing that we always need to guard against is that we are not putting all of our eggs into one basket. What do I mean by that? As frail human beings, we are prone to hope for things based on some unrealistic desire or information. As we have learned in previous chapters, hope is a God-given gift, but not a heavenly buffet of wishes granted as if we were children reaching out for a favorite toy.

In point of fact, we have already defined the differences between hope, wishes, and promises. It is over time that the wonderful power of hope becomes better understood. Only slowly is it possible for the real importance of hope to be found and embraced so that it becomes the hope that carries and sustains us in all manner of life's situations.

> *And not only that, but we also boast in our sufferings, knowing that suffering produces endurance, and endurance produces character, and character produces hope, and hope does not disappoint us, because God's love has been poured into our hearts through the Holy Spirit that has been given to us.* — Romans 5:3-5

It is inevitable that we will, as human beings, set our hope on that which is unrealistic and probably offers momentary satisfaction. Yet, as we have seen in the struggle of life, be it flying geese or people struggling to find fulfillment in life, the hope that God gives us will transform our lives in such a way that no quick fixes are seriously investigated.

However, in some ways, there is a paradox in all of this. The paradox is that hope, like seeds in the winter, must sometimes die in order to find life. Hope is often born out of the bleakest of circumstances. Probably the most visible example of this hope being born out of the bleakest of circumstances can be found in the apostle Peter.

Peter, as most of us know, stumbled from time to time. He, like most of us, was not a perfect person. In fact, Peter made some monumental errors in judgment and because of that he, more than most biblical characters, has become the standard for falling down and getting up again ready to go. This Peter, the one who fails and succeeds, is the one who shows us "the expectation of something yet to be."

Hope is a very necessary commodity for the well-being of human life. Admittedly, people are looking in a lot of wrong places to find hope in today's world. All you need to do is wait in line at the local convenience store while people spend their hard-earned money on lottery tickets to understand how desperate people are to find hope. People are always hoping that their ship is going to come in. Peter's life proves that just because hopes get crushed from time to time, does not mean that all hope has been lost.

> *Blessed be the God and Father of our Lord Jesus Christ! By his great mercy he has given us a new birth into a living hope through the resurrection of Jesus Christ from the dead, and into an inheritance that is imperishable, undefiled and unfading, kept in heaven for you.*
>
> — 1 Peter 1:3-4

Did you catch that? A living hope — a life-giving hope — a hope that is sure and steadfast that is rooted and grounded in a living relationship with God. Why is this hope labeled, "living"? It is because it is the true hope that comes from God. Too often, hope is placed in the wrong source. We place our hope in the things we hold dear, and that is just being human. For instance, we put our hope in ourselves; we put our hope in our partners; we put our hope in our work; we put our hope in our doctors; but ultimately, our hope will only come to life when it is first placed in the source of all hope, and that is Jesus Christ!

Hope finds expression in the "yet to be." Peter showed us through his life and the experiences of his life that are chronicled in the Bible, that hope has a life into the future. We have an inheritance of hope and that is gifted to us from God. It is an inheritance that we have not earned! That is the tremendous thing about hope, especially as it is given to us in Jesus Christ. We did nothing to earn or even deserve such hope. Maybe you have seen the bumper sticker that proclaims, "We're spending our children's inheritance." The interesting thing about the hope that God gives to us is that we can never, ever, spend it all! Imagine a hope that will last a lifetime and then an eternal lifetime.

It should be a comfort to us all that this hope will keep us going through any and all trials that may come our way. There are problems that lurk around every corner in every life. To my knowledge, we were never promised a life free of trouble. We all, no matter who we are or where we come from, get seduced into thinking that somehow we are going to get through life without hitting the speed bumps that accompany every life. We will have financial troubles; we will have people break promises or act terribly toward us; or, our children will not be perfect. Just because we think we have done the things we should have done to have a good life grants us no exemptions. Life is not easy.

All the trials that come that seem so insurmountable at the time, can be overcome. Those people who rub you the wrong way, those illnesses which debilitate you and rob you of strength, those losses that sadden you and madden you, may just be the process through which you travel to better appreciate the hope given us in Jesus Christ. Often it is in the midst of disappointments that hope shines the brightest. If all the trials of life make you angry, and you lose yourself in that anger, then hope is lost, or, at the very least, buried in your own misplaced sense of self. Because, you see, it is not God's intention that you be unhappy. God wants all of his creation to find itself in harmony with God and with one another. When we allow the disappointments of life to overcome us, we allow ourselves to extinguish the expectation of something in our lives that is yet to come to full growth and maturation.

The expectation of "something yet to be" is hope realized in the person of Jesus of Nazareth.

> *In this you rejoice, even if now for a little while you have had to suffer various trials, so that the genuineness of your faith, being more precious than gold that, though perishable, is tested by fire, may be found to result in praise and glory and honor when Jesus Christ is revealed.* — 1 Peter 1:6-7

We have not been blessed to have seen Jesus face-to-face, only through the eyes of hope and faith. We have the hope that we will see him face-to-face when that expectation of something yet to be comes into our eternal existence. But even now, without physically seeing him, we love him. There is a bottom line for the person who lives a Christian life. What does it mean to be a Christian? It means to love Jesus and to love God with all our hearts, minds, souls, and strength. It is to love him in spite of the fact that we have not seen him.

Down deep within the recesses of our souls a sense of joy is stored that cannot be removed and cannot be contained. It is a joy that is beyond natural; it is a joy that is beyond emotional; it is a joy that has been planted in our relationship with God, and nothing can destroy that which God has placed within us.

Those of us who call ourselves Christians should be the most joyous people on earth. Every part of our lives should radiate our joy at being part of the community of faith. Our hope should show through everything we do and say. Everything about us should speak to others about *whose* we are and *why* we are. It should tell others that we know that God loves us with an everlasting love, and that love can put a smile on anyone's face!

When we live our lives reflecting the expectation that good things will happen, we begin to live the life with which we have been gifted. It is a life where your actions and your words match. It is a life that says to anyone who will listen that we are filled with an "expectation of something yet to be!"

Questions For Your Consideration

1. What is the anticipation that having hope implies?

2. How do you find courage in hope? What are we to do with the courage we realize through hope?

3. In what ways are you and the apostle Peter alike? Find and discuss a biblical example that substantiates your thoughts.

4. What is paradoxical about hope?

5. How has life seduced you into thinking that you really were "better prepared for life" than you really are?

6. Look up John 14 and find the verses that give you an understanding of eternal hope as found in Jesus.

7. How do you manifest hope in your life of faith? How does that hope become visible?

8. How is it possible to love Jesus without ever having sat with him and talked with him one-on-one?

9. In your own life, how do others experience the hope you have in your life?

10. How can you help someone else to feel that same sense of hope in their life?

Chapter Four

Hope That Is Radical

When a Christian is asked, "Is hope real?" the answer should be apparent, but is it? Of course there is hope, but when one finds a need to ask the question, then obviously they are in a place where hope seems lost. For the married couple whose marriage seems to be falling apart, for the person who just cannot seem to break that addiction, for the expectant mother who hears the words, "I'm sorry, we simply cannot find a heart beat," where is hope? For the single parent trying to raise children alone, for the person who has been desperately seeking resolution to depression, for the person who is waiting at the hospice as the one they love slips slowly away, where is hope? Where is hope for the generation of today who has grown up in a world of drugs and violence?

As we have already seen in Peter's life, hope is radical. Hope comes to you when you least expect it! We are not talking about some otherworldly optimism that in the end everything will be all right. Because for many, hope is now and needs to manifest itself now. Our Christian hope is a hope that does not rest solely on humankind. This hope within us is hope that has been raised to life through our Lord Jesus Christ.

We need to look back in time to discover how this radical hope was embraced by the early church. It is astonishingly insightful to realize that these first Christians were able to find hope in a world in which they were the marginalized and the persecuted. The resurrection and all that it meant to the daily life of the early Christian cannot be underestimated. Human life and human history were altered in that one event. Hope itself became a force to be reckoned with as the early Christians set out to build a church.

The world in which the early church began to find life was a world of both opulence and poverty, not far different than our world today! While Greco-Roman civilization abounded with some of the greatest architectural monuments ever built, it floundered because it was not built on solid ground. The best and most powerful lived lives that mirror the lives of the rich and famous of our own world today. The Greco-Roman world had its advantages, to be sure. Those who were economically and politically well situated were able to live in a style that the majority of people could never envision.

But, despite what it all looked like on the outside, much of what they held dear was only as strong as their ability to control the world around them. Their hope was always in their own ability to conquer and to control. When threatened, there was only one good response and that was to crush whatever it was that was threatening them. You cannot crush the onslaught of age or the ravages of disease. When you have no hope at the end of life, you probably have had no hope in the life you are living.

To people who feel like they just cannot go on because they have no hope, a radical hope has been offered. In their hit record, "My Generation," the band the Who, echoed this feeling of despair when they sang that they hoped they would die before they got old. Youth has its place, but it is misplaced to believe you will always have it.

To everyone who has ever been overcome by feelings of worthlessness, God has opened the gates of hope through the life, ministry, death, and the resurrection of our Lord Jesus Christ. The resurrection is history's greatest sign of hope. It is this one event that changed everything in the world — everything! In the resurrection, God put the torch to a light that can never be extinguished! Without that light burning within the hearts of the early church, the church would not have survived the continuous onslaught of those who sought to destroy it. It is this resurrection hope that is still alive and active in the lives of the Christian community today.

Hope that is radical is hope alive! It is hope that finds expression in the living reality of a constant infusion of love that is freely given by the Son of God. God brought reconciliation to the world and sadly many did not, or would not, embrace it. The early church not only embraced it, but built upon it, because, unlike the Roman Empire, the early church found an assurance and pledge that the future would be filled with possibilities. They knew as we should also, that the future was to be faced with a sense of what can be, not any sense of what cannot be. There was no darkness that the light of Christ could not pierce.

This radical hope is so important today because in so many ways, hope seems to be mired in a slow process of decay. We all need to be able to look courageously in the eye of the clouds of what the world says cannot be and find within those clouds the everlasting light of Christ our Lord. This is a living, breathing, life-giving hope that can transcend the many negative forces that always seem to be trying to undo that which is good and helpful and healing in our world. Our future is not in the hands of fate or destiny, it is in the hands of God. It is easy for us to become lackadaisical about our place in the universe. We may be disappointed about the way we mess up and find ourselves the cause of another's despair. We may become dejected about an illness or a failed business venture or some family problem, but, in the end, our disappointment will always be usurped by the hope that has been radicalized in Jesus Christ.

A note of caution is in place here. In no way do I wish to minimize the very real pain and anguish felt by so many for very good reasons. I would never belittle the agony in mind or body that many people live with daily. But the Christian has something that others may not have. They can have confidence and trust in God that the future is firm and that God will not falter in caring for us, no matter what.

Let's face it, we do not know what life has in store for us. If we did, we could plan accordingly and try to avoid the pitfalls of living life in a world filled with uncertainty. Fortunately, we have a confident knowledge that God loves us and that God ultimately cares for us now and forever. We have that living hope because we have a living Savior who is able to sympathize with us because he has felt the pain we feel and knows the inner workings of our hearts. None of us will ever have complete freedom from the problems of this life while we are living it. Each of us will have personal struggles with one thing or another that will be with us until the day we die. There will always be something that will remind us that we live life on the edge of hope and despair. Luckily for us, hope has already won the race.

The apostle Paul put it this way.

> *We are afflicted in every way, but not crushed; perplexed, but not driven to despair; persecuted, but not forsaken; struck down, but not destroyed; always carrying in the body the death of Jesus, so that the life of Jesus may also be made visible in our mortal flesh.*
>
> — 2 Corinthians 4:8-12

It is this hope that allows us to put perspective into the troubles that we will face in life. What can be seen is only a momentary reality, but the joy of heaven is forever! It is with that knowledge in mind that we can face the day-to-day situations that we all must live with. It has everything to do with what is on the inside and very little to do with what is showing on the outside. Again, refer back to the early church leaders who built what we inherited as the Christian church. It was an inner strength that allowed them to see hope when all around them was darkness. Where did these people find the courage to do the things they did? It is no easy matter to live life knowing that each day may be your last because of your beliefs. Where did the everyday woman and man find the direction they needed to spread the gospel and build the church? It is easy for us to point to Peter and the other famous church leaders, because we have records of their faithful journeys into the unknown. But what of the butcher, the baker, and the candlestick maker? How were they able to stand up against incredible odds and proclaim their faith and build the church in the face of death?

These people were able to do what they did because they lived in the shadow of the eternal. They lived with a living Lord! They didn't hope for the sake of hoping. Their hope was radical in that it was a hope based on an internal change that happened in their lives. We who live on this side of the resurrection can be filled with the same hope that filled those early church leaders. Yes, some of them walked with Jesus before and after the resurrection. But we have their eyewitness accounts to base our hope upon and that is as solid a foundation as we will ever find.

Our life situations may change, but that change, whatever it may be, need not hinder our hopeful life. The reason is simple:

Real hope, radical hope, resurrection hope is not about changing what is happening in our day-to-day living; it is about allowing God to change what is going on inside of us! And how can we be a part of bringing about that hope within our daily living? Let us take a look back in church history. Early Christians were characterized by their energy and open spirit of hope. It was a spirit of triumph and a spirit of life everlasting. Their worship and their work were done in a spirit of anticipation and joy. In a very real sense, they were already experiencing in their lives what it meant to be a resurrection people.

Just imagine what this kind of living looked like to those who were first encountering these Christians, these new Christians. Their way of living made those around them curious about what it was that led them into this life of hopeful living. They were mistreated because of what they believed; they were the target of government and religious persecution. But, instead of becoming bitter and filled with hatred, they did what they had been taught to do by Jesus, they turned their persecution into an opportunity to tell the world the good news that had changed their lives. This was strange behavior to those in positions of power. The center of their lives was a hopeful outlook on what would one day come to be. Any momentary slow down in the spreading of the greatest story ever told was simply an opportunity to become centered again and focus in on the work that was to be done.

The reality for these early Christians was that no matter what was happening at that time, the best was yet to come! They knew and lived life as people who had their eyes on something much more significant than some partial material gain while on this side of eternity. Their eyes were set on the final hope that awaits all. Their hope and ours is secure in the understanding that we will experience such joy when we are in the presence of Jesus that momentary misery now is only a fait and fading pain as compared to the glory yet to come. As Paul wrote so eloquently, "For now we see in a mirror, dimly, but then we will see face to face. Now I know only in part; then I will know fully, even as I have been fully known" (1 Corinthians 13:12).

Questions For Your Consideration

1. Describe why someone would think that having hope is a radical idea.

2. Where and how do we learn to hold onto hope, when everything around us points to a reality that there is no hope at all?

3. How is the world of the twenty-first century similar to the world the early church lived in?

4. How did Jesus' life translate into hope for the early church? Explain this in light of the fact that Jesus did not come back as was expected.

5. What has to happen inside of a person to make that person a person filled with hope?

6. How does the idea of eternity fit into the idea of a hope-filled life?

7. Can we change the world we live in without first changing ourselves?

8. Why can't we change the world we live in without first changing ourselves?

9. When beset by trouble, how can you rediscover the hope that Jesus showed in his life, death, and resurrection?

10. What and where is the mirror that the apostle Paul spoke of in 1 Corinthians 13?

Chapter Five

Our Hope Is A Forever Thing!

A little girl lived near a cemetery and often had to walk through it after dark. When someone asked her about being afraid in such a place, she answered, "Oh, no! My hope is just on the other side."

The best way to describe, or to detail, what the little girl was talking about, is to first ask a question, "Do you think that your home, your eternal home, is just on the other side?" Is your hope a forever thing? Does your sense of hope extend beyond the boundaries that we set for ourselves in this material world? As you walk through the valley of the shadow of death, do you, or do you not, fear what is on the other side of that valley? Our hope as Christians is not only that we will reach the other side, our hope resides in the one who will hold our hand on the journey.

Our world is filled with pie-in-the-sky ideas of what may be. With the dearth of new age religions or simply new age thinking comes a sort of spiritual blindness that may even seem like a good thing. Spiritual blindness means you never have to see what is right in front of your face. It means finding temporary bliss in the here and now and never fully coming to grips with the here-and-there part of life. But, it all comes down to knowing that when your journey is complete you will continue walking hand in hand with the one who came to give us life and that, eternally, is Jesus Christ our Savior. Intimately, without that eternal assurance our hope would be without foundation.

It is so easy to get caught up in thinking that we will be one with the cosmos — that maybe we will come back in another form in another life. Or conversely, that when we finally end our life's journey, we are dust and nothing more. In fact, that is the blindness that has already been mentioned. It is easier on an intellectual level to simply be convinced that when you die, you're food for the worms. If that is true, then you need not worry about how you live your life among the living. You could pretty much do and say whatever you wished because in the end all there would be was the end!

Christian hope gives us a different and much more meaningful interpretation of life now and forever. Christian hope says that a man by the name of Jesus came into the world, lived, died, was resurrected, and came to tell us about "the other side" that the little girl spoke of. Only one person has ever been there and done that, and that person tells us that we can expect the same thing in our eternal life. Only Jesus, and no other, has ever even claimed such a thing. Indeed, resurrection is that one thing that separates Christianity from all the other religions in the world.

In Paul's letter to the church in Corinth, chapter 15, he speaks to some in that early church who say there is no resurrection. Paul understands fully that without that firm foundational belief the early church will stumble and fail. The early church would lose hope! Paul, understanding the eternal consequences of this mistaken notion, asks this knowing full well that these people carry with them their own history, their own set of beliefs that were in place long before they ever heard a word about Jesus. Not only that, but these same people lived in a city and in a world that was filled with alternate ways of living and believing.

It is truly difficult to paint an accurate picture of what Paul and the other early church leaders faced when they first converted these early followers. Remember that for some, religion was based upon the satisfying of their earthly needs first. For others, the idea of such a dreadful thing as sacrificing children did not seem all that bad! Some thought that temple prostitutes were a necessary part of religion. In other words, they brought the word of the Prince of Peace into a world that more than likely thought it all sounded a little too good to be true. They may have considered Christianity a way of addressing how to live a more normal life.

The more you look at it, the more you understand the people and times, and the more you can see analogies to our world today. There is no question that almost all people in our country, if not most of the world, have at least heard of Jesus. But, it is not fair to say that they have understood the hope that is found in his ministry. Into this complex world, Christ was introduced and it is in this complex world that Paul raises the question, "What if there is no resurrection?" What would it mean to be a Christian without the resurrection and the hope that is such an integral part of being a follower of Jesus? What would the church mean without the resurrection? What if there was no hope of a resurrection?

First of all, all the focus of a people without the hope of resurrection must be centered on the things that are right in front of you. Since there is no hope for anything after death, then Christianity is reduced to being a religion that needs to provide something to satisfy your hunger today. What is it that Christianity can provide today that will make my day better and will assure me that it will happen again tomorrow? Again, these same questions are germane to our world today in the twenty-first century.

Hopeful people have a place to live. A simple statement, but an essential element to life. The most logical place to start in terms of a place to be, is the building of a church, a house dedicated to the God they were going to worship. In the world in which there is no resurrection, this house would have to be pretty impressive. The building would have to compete with the other houses of worship that people attend. The larger the congregation, the larger the need would be to have a structure that would show the world how important this religion was and therefore, how important were the people who came to this house to worship. This house would be in direct competition with the other places that served the same purpose and because there would be no hope of resurrection, we would constantly need to be upgrading the building with all the latest "stuff" so as to impress visitors and neighbors. We would need better music than the competition and when necessary, we would have to adjust our thinking. More to the point, we would have to insure that our philosophy met with the approval of more than that of our competitors. In essence, we would need to provide a place of comfort and personal satisfaction, so that members would stay and new people would be impressed enough to come and join us.

Another important factor in our no-resurrection world would be that we would need to have good and easy-to-follow rules. These rules would have to be flexible because people would move to the place where the rules best suited their lifestyles. For some, the rules would be pretty strict, for others, not so much. Elasticity of these rules would become absolutely essential. A person may prefer a church where musical instruments were encouraged, or conversely where no musical instruments would be tolerated. But none of these decisions would be based on solid convictions. This would be all there was. There would be no real ramifications for the things we said or did, so why worry about being in compliance with a set of rules? Why worry?

For example, if there is no hope beyond today, why worry about how we treat one another? If my father has become old and difficult to care for, why worry about it? Without the resurrection we would never see one another again, so why should I go out of my way caring for him? My hope is based on what is happening today, so if the old man has no hope, that is not my problem. You see, without hope, our responsibility to our sisters and brothers in creation becomes a pick-and-choose kind of event in life. If the person in question can do us some good, then maybe that person should be taken care of.

On the other hand, if the person is of no consequence, then like the traveler on the road who passes by the man in the ditch, we also pass by without pause or worry. The question becomes: Without any sense of hope, what am I willing to do to get what I want in life? If there is no resurrection, then when it comes right down to it, the only consequences I bring upon myself are those I wish to have as part of my life. In fact, if there is no resurrection, then who cares?

To take it to an extreme, without hope without a sense of possible ramifications good or bad for my future, why not just kill people I don't like? Conversely, when I have hope, when I understand that Jesus is with me all the way, I will treat people as if I am going to spend an eternity with them! What an enormous change that would bring into all facets of life. All of our decisions would then be made in the light of Easter morning.

Listen to what Paul said about this subject. Please remember that when Paul wrote these things, he was writing them to people who could easily have refuted his claims, had his claims not be factual.

Now if Christ is proclaimed as raised from the dead, how can some of you say there is no resurrection of the dead? If there is no resurrection of the dead, then Christ has not been raised; and if Christ has not been raised, then our proclamation has been in vain and your faith has been in vain. We are even found to be misrepresenting God, because we testified of God that he raised Christ whom he did not raise if it is true that the dead are not raised. For if the dead are not raised, then Christ has not been raised. If Christ has not been raised, your faith is futile and you are still in your sins. Then those also who have died in Christ have perished. If for this life only we have hoped in Christ, we are of all people most to be pitied.

But in fact, Christ has been raised from the dead, the first fruits of those who have died.

— 1 Corinthians 15:12-20

There are many biblical and historical texts that must be taken into consideration when talking about the resurrection. For any person to simply dismiss them out of hand is ignorant! Paul, in verses just quoted, sets forth a well-thought-out argument. Intended to both stimulate and challenge anyone who would deny the reality of the resurrection. This is an argument that intended to set the stage for any future challenge.

Those who were out to prove that Jesus was just another carpenter never actually challenged the resurrection itself. They said that Jesus' disciples had taken his body from the tomb to make it look like he had been raised. By saying that, they affirmed that the tomb was indeed empty. But when you think about it, would it not have made more sense for them to go and open the tomb themselves? But that did not happen. If they really believed that the disciples had stolen the body, then why did they not have the disciples arrested and have their homes searched for the body? Why not encourage Pilate and his troops to torture them until they told the truth that they wanted to hear? But that was never done!

Our resurrection hope helps us to see through the smoke screens that are set up by those who wanted then, and still want today, to convince us that Jesus did not rise from that rocky cave.

When we speak of hope, we have to talk about those who authored the gospels. What about these people? If they were trying to deceive people, they certainly could have done a better job of it. If the story of Jesus is nothing more than a fabricated tale told to fool people, the story would have been much more colorful and filled with many more exciting details.

When you think about it, what good writer of fiction would not include at least one person who could be put on the stand and be a credible witness? You know, someone who could talk about thunder rumbling so loudly that it shook the ground, or a blinding light from the sky, or angels singing while God spoke and Jesus emerged from his tomb? A true weaver of words would most certainly have had Jesus appear first to the person designated to build the church: Peter. And, if not Peter, then John, but not a reformed prostitute, Mary Magdalene, in the quiet of the garden.

Doesn't it make more sense to think that one of the disciples would be sharpening his sword in anticipation of the battle to come? This is all to say that the gospels, in and of themselves, do not offer the kind of descriptive scenes one would have thought would have been present in such a dramatic story. If the gospel writers wanted to prove the resurrection, they could have done so simply by painting a much more descriptive picture of the event that has shaped the world as we know it.

The hope found in the resurrection of Jesus comes to us despite our misgivings, whatever they may be. Hope and resurrection go hand in hand. Jesus' resurrection assures us of our own new day, our day of hope, and that is eternal. "But now Christ has been raised from the dead, the firstfruits of those who are asleep" (1 Corinthians 15:20).

Talk about hope, can there be any greater hope than that found in the promise of life eternal? It is important to understand that this hope is not like waiting for something to happen. It is, rather, a hope which is also an assurance, a confidence, found in the risen Lord, both now and forever.

Questions For Your Consideration

1. Describe your sense of what, if anything, happens following death.

2. How does the resurrection influence you in your day-to-day living?

3. How, if at all, does hope and eternal life change your view of other religions that do not adhere to the same beliefs as we, who call ourselves Christians?

4. What qualities do you think are given to humankind because of the resurrection?

5. How do you think a lack of hope can change a person or nation?

6. Conversely, how does hope influence the individual who finally embraces that hope, particularly if that person is a Christian?

7. Do you have to be Christian to have hope?

8. Why did the apostle Paul go out of his way to remind people that without the resurrection there is no life?

9. Are the gospel accounts believable because they are accurate, or are they believable because they are true?

10. Define what the resurrection means in terms of how it influences hope.

Chapter Six

Hope And The Power Of God's Presence

We must all come to terms with the reality that we can never understand the meaning of hope if that understanding is based on our own achievements or lack thereof. Arrogance would have us believe that we can do remarkable things and take credit for those things without any regard for the working of God in those achievements. We are reminded over and over again that we do not need God. Advertisements are full of veiled messages that *we* are the center of the universe, and that we should trust only in our own ability to care for ourselves and the world we live in. But leaving God behind communicates to all that we can bring God into our lives anytime we wish. Indeed, it says that God is at our bidding and will do as we wish, when we wish.

Nowhere in that kind of thinking does the idea that it is God who comes to us come into focus. In reality, we are not dealing with only our own wit and strength. We are, instead, dealing with the very author of life. Our hope should never be based on our own ability to handle life, it should be based on the reality that God never ceases to be present and we do nothing without God at our side! The prophet Isaiah identified this fact when he wrote, "The Lord of hosts has sworn: As I have designed, so shall it be; and as I have planned, so shall it come to pass" (Isaiah 14:24). Any understanding of hope will wither and simply fall away when you most need it, if you do not acknowledge that our hope is found in the Lord of hosts.

The issue is not our coming to God, it is God's coming to us. We all need to better understand that when God became one of us in Jesus Christ, God was showing all of creation the incredible depth and the love that God has for all of us, no matter who we may be. We cannot even begin to truly comprehend the power of that kind of love. It is the power of light over darkness, it is the power of knowing joy when joy seems lost, and it is the power of life over death. It is the power of hope.

When we begin to grasp what God has done for us in the incarnation, we begin to better appreciate the life over death love that God has for us all. It is through God's coming to us that God offers to us a new way of thinking and a new way of imagining our lives, present and future. If God could divinely enter life in the person of Jesus of Nazareth, why do we find it so hard to come to the point of understanding that because of God's coming in human form, we who hold that human form no longer have to fear death?

One of the best ways to discover why our hope is found in Jesus Christ is best understood when we delve into the pages of the gospel of John. Verses 1-18 of this wonderful gospel offer us linguistic images that open up new possibilities in our journey of faith. Indeed, it is within the pages of John's gospel that we begin to see the profound impact that these words hold for us. Those words, so eloquently penned by John, can shape our entire outlook on life. Our own sense of what it means to be a Christian can be greatly enhanced by these wonderful words of life. One of the most compelling reasons is that John, unlike the other gospel writers, tells us that the power of God's love preexisted all of life as we know it. "In the beginning was the Word, and the Word was with God, and the Word was God" (John 1:1). Wow, that should get your attention.

John is saying that all of that power that preexisted is available to all of us! It is saying that this wonderful power has been made attainable for us in the person of Jesus Christ. Just think about that for a moment. "And the Word became flesh and dwelt among us" (John 1:14). "He was in the world, and the world was made through him, yet the world knew him not. He came to his own home and his own people received him not" (John 1:10-11). Further, regardless of the fact that his own neighbors rejected him, the power of eternal love prevailed and always will throughout all of time. "The light shines in the darkness, and the darkness has not overcome it" (John 1:5).

Hope does not rely on our feeble attempts to validate what it is. The power of light over darkness stands at the heart of hope. We have a hope-filled future because God took us and shaped us and loved us enough to change us into the hopeful people we were created to be.

As a pastor, I try to remind myself daily that hope is a power that is real and available to me. When circumstances seem to suggest that someone or some plan has fallen upon difficult times and it seems as if all hope is lost, I slow down and try to tap into the light of hope. I remind myself that I can never be invulnerable to the things that plague us all, most of the time. Pain and tragedy are a part of life, but so is the reality of God. I will still be vulnerable to pain; but I will not be beaten back into a weakened state. I will not feel defeated because my hope is not confined only to my present situation, my hope is more dynamic than some frail definition I may come up with.

When you look at this hope, this divine promise, you begin to see that even Jesus was brought face-to-face with the reality of hopelessness. As a man, Jesus could be and was humiliated, tortured, and finally executed like a common criminal. But as a child of God, he was invincible, he was quite literally above it all, by the power of God. Therefore, any true understanding of the life and ministry of Jesus himself must start with the power of a loving God that was made perfect in weakness! We may call it hopelessness in our world today, but there can be hope even in the midst of pain. It is always difficult to find it when we are hurting, but it is there and that is the promise God has given us in Christ Jesus our Lord.

The gospel of John presents to us a remarkable view of our Savior. It is a view that is unique when compared with the synoptic gospels. It is a view that tells us that God took time to come into our world and that God pitched a tent and lived with us in all facets of our lives. It is through this selfless act that we begin to grasp that in this act of giving, God showed us that God is available to us in the ordinary living of our lives. God made Jesus present to us as a matter of free will. Nothing has been forced upon us. We did nothing to entice God to do what was done. God saw our inability to deal with life in a constructive way and God freely chose to come and share our life.

Time and time again we need to remind ourselves that God came to us, we did nothing to force God to come and be with us. Isn't it true that when someone volunteers to be part of something, that act of volunteering makes that person an energetic participant because no force was leveled against that person to make them become part of whatever it is we are doing? That voluntary act of giving of oneself makes everything else pale in significance. God came to us in Jesus, knowing full well that that act of coming would bring with it times of pain and struggle. That is why Jesus stuck around when the going got rough. It was his idea to be with us in the first place! I would suggest that Jesus' presence and power was increased simply by his act of voluntarily giving of himself on our behalf.

I think it is fair to say that there is a discernible difference between caring for somebody because it is our job and caring for someone because we know in our hearts that caring is exactly what God would have us do. Most people instinctively know the difference. Walk into any nursing home or hospital and you will be able to discern without much trouble who is caring from the heart and who is caring because of the money. You can be sure that the residents and patients know who is doing what and why.

Our hope can also be found in the fact that God comes into our lives without strings attached. It is sometimes said that everything in life has some precondition to it, but not with God. Some people do project that God should insist on some minimal requirements, but that is not the biblical picture with which we are presented. Indeed, it is the fact that we have to lose our preconditions for God's love that is the most hopeful ingredient in God's coming. It matters not who or where you are from; it matters not from whom or from where your money comes; it matters not how, where, or from whom your religion comes; that is why hope is so very real!

If, as John writes in his gospel, "the Word was with God, and the Word was God," there were no strings attached. God had nothing to gain by coming into our lives and putting up with the pain of our lives. God had nothing to gain by being humiliated and having to endure the indignities that are so human. And that is all the more remarkable and all the more hopeful for all of us, because it is we, after all, who bring the humility upon God! Once again, God shows the power of his love in life, and even in death, through example.

I don't believe that we could ever find a better foundation on which to build our hope. Just think how lucky we are. Think about the two most visible reasons for us to find hope in God's activity in Christ. God's love and God's power have been given visible forms in the person of Jesus of Nazareth. These extraordinary powers, love and power itself, are given clarity for anyone who will pay attention. In the life, death, and resurrection of Jesus, we are granted eternal sight into the life of hope.

Let me raise a possible problem with all of this. The problem is that although God never stops loving us and never stops offering hope to us, we are not so inclined. We are much more likely to forsake God than God is to forsake us! We are much more likely to deny God's love and power than God is to give it. For reasons that seem to reach back into history, we have the sad tendency to be hopeless even in the face of all that God has and continues to do for us. The main reason seems to be that we, frail as we are, are still fragile, self-centered humans, looking for something we cannot even define. We want the world handed to us on a silver platter and we experience a loss of hope when we don't get what we want fast enough. The sad truth is that, when faced with a problem, the first place we turn is not to God, it is usually to the world around us. We will turn to new age gurus whose books fill the shelves of our local bookstores. We will turn to drugs and alcohol before we turn to God. It is not that we don't know any better, we do! But, our human weakness is to try to find the quickest fix, and when that fails, we turn to God, or worse yet, we begin to blame God for whatever it is that is ailing us.

Sin has been defined by some as a turning away from God and a turning instead to yourself. We begin to blame God for the things that we cannot control. The problem arises when, in our search for hope, we refuse to accept God's free gifts and instead decide that we can, in and of ourselves, solve the problems that are taking a toll upon our lives. The sad reality is that as long as we are dependent on our own power, we are running headlong into our own day of hopeless despair. No matter how many academic degrees we hang on our walls, no matter how much money we have in the bank, it is impossible for us to live without sinning. That being the case, our only hope is in a strength far beyond ourselves. Hope and sin may seem very strange companions, but they are not. The apostle Paul reminds us, "For I do not do what I want, but I do the very thing I hate" (Romans 7:15). It is because of this fact, so clearly articulated by Paul, that we can better understand that living life without making mistakes is not possible. Therefore, hope is to be found outside of our own feeble attempts to live believing we can fix anything, anytime, without God's presence.

Questions For Your Consideration

1. How does the advertising world communicate to us that we are able to do whatever we want whenever we want?

2. The reading from Isaiah tells us that God has our lives all planned. Do you believe this?

3. How do you see God coming into your life each day? Why do you not feel God in your life each day?

4. Turn to chapter 1 of John in your Bibles. Read verses 1-18 and explain how they help you know that hope is real.

5. Why do you think God saw a need to come into your life in the first place?

6. What strings do you think are attached to your life when you rely only upon yourself to live life?

7. Power and love are attributes that most people want to have in their lives. How are these powers manifest in Jesus' coming into the world?

8. How does hope find life within the constraints of family, work, and your own personal "baggage," whatever it may be?

9. What do you think Paul was talking about in Romans 7:15?

10. What does it mean to you to know that Jesus was present when the world was created? How does that help or hinder your feelings of hope?

Chapter Seven

Hopeful Understanding

Every time our human will trumps our need to discover God's will, we are in trouble. Hope is always rooted in faith, and like faith, hope is ultimately a response to the one who comes to speak a word of grace, and in that word to bring again the confidence that through the darkness there will always be a light at the end of the tunnel. Jesus brought that word and through that word brought us a new perspective on hope and on how to live a hope-filled life.

Sin is a part of life. For most people, the word "sin" is really easy to understand. There are many very complicated definitions of what sin is and how sin impacts our lives. But, sin is, at the most foundational point, our estrangement from God. It is most easily summarized in the image we are given from Sunday school to Bible study: one bite of one apple! Still, it is critical to understand that it is not the bite, but the thought behind the bite that is the sin. Why did human creation take that apple and bite into it? Why couldn't we enjoy our presence in God's perfect presence? You would think that would be enough to satisfy anyone.

Again, once we take the apple, we are taking our own initiative and leaving God in the background of our lives. We wanted then, and most of us want now, to be given access to the tree of knowledge. We desire to know what God knows and we desire to be able to act on that knowledge. It is that desire that we call sin. We think that once we have the knowledge of God we can then be God! Once we discover the freedom to act as we want, we have made contact with the root of the tree of knowledge, and that root is disobedience to the one who created the tree in the first place.

In his book, *The Ethics of Freedom*, author, Jacques Ellul writes:

> *The moment I am aware of myself I become the unique central and essential person who lies beyond everything. Only my own destiny concerns me. For I am the central thing in the world. We thus see the dawn of*

> *pride, egotism, and also of worry and anxiety. For if the self is the center of all things, if everything begins with me, then how can I avoid the anguished realization that everything also ends with me?*[1]

In order for a person to understand sin and why sin robs us of hope, a person must first feel what it is to sin. One cannot be sorry for sin if one does not shoulder responsibility for whatever misdeed has been done. The question arises: Does the person assume any responsibility or does the person present himself or herself as the victim of circumstances? This is usually the case when someone says that it was really external circumstances that caused that person to do whatever it is that needs forgiveness. In other words, is he or she the passive victim, or worse yet, is the person filled with rage and looking for revenge? Where is hope to be found when the idea of sin is simply ignored, or worse yet, used as a defense?

You see, we all know that we need to assume responsibility if we have done something wrong. But, one must not think that they need to carry a burden that is larger than the problem. In this case, the person could lose hope in the future. Does remorse lead automatically to repentance? Remorse, regret, and sorrow are the feelings that usually end up in the mind of the one doing the sinning. The truth of the matter is that unless the person who is feeling that remorse sets things right with the one who has been the victim, they will never feel the release of the burden of whatever sin has been committed. It is sort of like John the Baptist's cry from the River Jordan, "Repent." But, to repent means that the person has to engage in the act or repentance. That repentance should result in a constructive ending to the problem.

One of the best ways to find that kind of repentance is through what the church has come to call "community." I do not mean community only in the religious sense of the word, rather, I mean that humble, compassionate, and heartfelt sense of communion that allows a person to say, "We are all in this together." Or in the language of the church, "We are all poor sinners," or, in our common vernacular, "We all make mistakes, some of them whoppers!" But, even when I do make a whopper of a mistake, I have the comfort of knowing that I belong to a community of people who will allow me to come back and will help me to heal.

The first position we may call "being continuous" and the opposite of that would be discontinuous. That would mean, once again, that a person finds themselves without any visible means of support. It is the position of one who has lost any hope that they can no longer be part of the larger community. They believe this because they think that they have committed something that will, in the end, separate them from the community that once was home. Sadly, some folks are comfortable living without support, but most of us find healing and hope when we are embraced and forgiven.

Hope allows the discontinuous person, the one who feels separated from the community, to step back into the community and feel the strength of community versus the lack of strength that is felt when one isolates and becomes truly alone in their remorse. That hope can only be found in the person's willingness to become a humble creature, and let God be God.

The people who have withdrawn, who have lost that sense of being part of something larger than themselves, become only a shadow of who they really are. In their zeal to separate themselves because of their fear of facing sin, they have created a kingdom that cannot be maintained without losing their own sense of self. It is a kingdom that is doomed to fall because it is not built upon a firm foundation, and that foundation is Jesus Christ.

When we rely on the world, we are inviting disaster into our personal world. When the whole world is viewed as a personal pacifier, the smallest rejection becomes a weight too large to carry. I would suggest that if anything stands in the way of hope, it is the nearsighted notion discussed previously that the future depends on us; it is the far-flung dream that we are in charge of tomorrow; it is the nagging feeling that we are unable to cope with today, let alone learn to live in the world we have created tomorrow!

The fact of the matter is that isolation often becomes painful because of a sense of guilt and shame. Most people, most of the time, know when they are doing something that is not going to prove constructive in the day-to-day living of their lives.

I remember on more than one occasion listening to troubled parishioners as they explained that they had everything, yet felt as if they had nothing. The more they accumulated, the more they felt distanced from reality. There was an emptiness present that could not be filled with "stuff." It is an emptiness that is a symptom of a loss of hope that life has more meaning than all that stuff.

Hope means that we know deep down in our souls that there really is something else besides all of the things that the world tells us we need or that the world tells us we cannot live without. Hope tells us that when all the trimmings are pushed aside, when all the *stuff* truly becomes nothing more than a momentary satisfaction, there is still something to live for. Hope tells us that we are more than a camouflaged image of Madison Avenue advertising. Hope allows us to rediscover ourselves if for some reason we have become lost in the world.

If and when hope seems lost, it may be time to redefine your lifestyle. Is there a reason for your loss of hope? Is it because as discussed above you have become hostage to other things that seem important, but offer no real comfort in life? If that is the case, it may just be time for you to focus all of your energy on something or someone outside of yourself. It may be time to consider immersing yourself into some project or person who will remove you from worrying about yourself. Take time to write down how you spend your time and see if there is a way to refocus your time and energy in some kind of project that will benefit someone other than yourself. Remember the words of Jesus, "He who finds his life will lose it, and he who loses his life for my sake will find it."

Let the following story serve to illustrate the point. The devil was having a yard sale, and all of his tools were marked with different prices. The tools up for sale were as varied as the people who were searching for that one tool that would help them build the life they wanted. There was a tool labeled hatred, another was lust, and deceit, lying, and pride. All of the tools were priced very high. But on a separate table, off to the side, was a tool that had obviously been used many times over. Although it was worn more than any of the others, it was the highest priced item for sale. The tool was labeled, "discouragement."

When asked why this particular tool was so highly priced, the devil gave his very best devilish smile, and answered, "It's more useful to me than any other tool for sale. When I can't bring my victims down with any of these other tools, I use discouragement, because most of them don't even realize it belongs to me."

You see, it is when hope seems lost or simply beyond our grasp that we need to reflect on why that is. Has discouragement set in to the point at which we cannot find hope, even when others are able? Maybe it is time to use the gifts God has blessed you with to the advantage of others. How you use those gifts will determine, to a large degree, how you will rediscover the hope that has been lost. In our world today, many people say, "I hope so," in such a way that what they are really saying is, "I doubt it." The New Testament translates the word "hope" as "confident expectation." For the Christian, hope carries with it the connotation of an expected result, without doubt. And God has been preparing you to use that confident expectation all your life.

God often gives hope as a precursor to living out the possibility of God's gifts in your life. Remember Abraham? He is surrounded by idolatry and wickedness. God gives Abraham a very special promise.

> *Now the LORD had said to Abram, "Get out of your country, from your family and from your father's house to a land that I will show you. I will make you a great nation; I will bless you and make your name great; and you shall be a blessing. I will bless those who bless you, and I will curse him who curses you; and in you all the families of the earth shall be blessed."*
>
> — Genesis 12:1-3 (NKJV)

Abraham's wife, Sarah, was up until that time unable to have children. And God uses that fact as an opportunity to show Abraham new hope in his life by this great message, "I will make you a great nation; I will bless you and make your name great." How many think you might be excited about life if you had just gotten a promise from God like that? It provided Abraham with the strength he needed to do what God had in mind for him to do.

And Abraham ran into more than his share of discouragements. When he got to the land God had promised him, he found that there were already people there. The Canaanites were living in the land that Abraham thought was to be his. What did God do? He told Abraham, in no uncertain terms, that his offspring and their offspring after them would live in that land. Then there came famine in the exact location God had told him to go. Remember, discouragement? I don't know about you, but if God led me somewhere, I would expect things to be in pretty good condition upon my arrival. Abraham went to Egypt and had a moral failure, telling Sarah to lie about her being his wife. And you know, our own failures always seem much worse than the failures of others. In fact, our own failures end up being our greatest discouragements.

What did God do to help Abraham succeed in his journey? On a number of different occasions, God fed Abraham's soul with reminders of God's promise. And why did God do that? Because hope is what gave Abraham the strength he needed to get the job done.

In order to claim hope, we must overcome those things in our life that separate us from God's loving-kindness. We must continually be aware of God's presence and not be afraid to stay in that presence, as Paul Tournier writes:

> *The strong have learned how to play their hand so as to win in the game of life, and they become prisoners of the game. If we are to be strong we must simplify life, shutting our eyes to its disturbing complexity. Thus the strong quickly become the prisoners of a systematizing habit of mind and a simplistic philosophy which ends by drying them up and cutting them off from life.*[2]

The apostle Paul would explain things by saying that we must come to understand that we are in trouble as long as we are in what he called the "flesh," meaning we are all wrapped up within our selves. He would strongly suggest that we find a way to surrender our own will to God's will and in that process find the hope we need to continue our journey of faith.

---

1. Jacques Ellul, *The Ethics of Freedom* (Grand Rapids: Wm. B. Eerdmans, 1987), p. 136.

2. Paul Tournier, *The Strong and the Weak* (Philadelphia: Westminster Press, 1963), p. 169.

Questions For Your Consideration

1. Define sin as you have discovered it in your own life.

2. The story of creation has a tree of knowledge that was off limits to Adam and Eve. Why do you think they could not resist that tree? Where is that tree in our lives today?

3. What is the difference between being the victim of circumstances and owning up to our misdeed whatever it may be?

4. Have you ever felt lost? How has that feeling manifested itself within your interactions with others?

5. How does the church turn away people who have lost hope? Who are these people?

6. What can you do to redefine the way you live as a means of helping yourself or another find hope that seems lost?

7. Are there times you feel like Abraham? How does God show you the promised land?

8. Talk about the things in your life that keep you from living life the way you really would like to live it.

9. Can hope be manufactured, or is it a God-given gift that needs to be unwrapped in order to appreciate?

10. What is the fleshiest part of your life? How can you discard that "flesh" from your day-to-day living?

Chapter Eight

Hope: Jesus — And God's Loving Concern

We have established that hope goes hand in hand with a sense of knowing oneself. In fact, hope also carries with it a certain amount of humility, especially at that time in life when we recognize that we are not the center of the universe. The Christian community has found in a very personal way that the hope we claim can only be claimed because of the fact that Jesus totally denied himself for us. He, in a very real way, appeared to be in a hopeless situation, when, in fact, hope is most visible in his death! We can say that because it was at Calvary that Jesus totally denied himself on our behalf. It follows then, that when the self is denied, darkness seems to surround us, but it is in the midst of that darkness that the light begins to shine. It is as if God was trying to tell us, "When you put yourself down, I will pick you up!"

If you were a theological student, what I am talking about would be called, "justification by grace." This is one of those foundational underpinnings that is a central part of who we are as Christians. It was possibly the most important part of the great reformer, Martin Luther's, theology. The apostle Paul summarized this idea in the following way.

> *They must not speak evil of anyone, and they must avoid quarreling. Instead, they should be gentle and show true humility to everyone. Once we, too, were foolish and disobedient. We were misled by others and became slaves to many wicked desires and evil pleasures. Our lives were full of evil and envy. We hated others, and they hated us.*
>
> *But then God our Savior showed us his kindness and love. He saved us, not because of the good things we did, but because of his mercy. He washed away our sins and gave us a new life through the Holy Spirit. He*

generously poured out the Spirit upon us because of what Jesus Christ our Savior did. He declared us not guilty because of his great kindness. And now we know that we will inherit eternal life. — Titus 3:2-7

Why was this idea of "justification by grace" such an important part of Martin Luther's theology and what part does it play in our having a hope-filled life?

It has to do with much of what has been said thus far. We try and try to do and imagine things that are goal-oriented and people-generated. In other words, we want that apple and we want that tree and we want to do it because we can! But can we? The answer to that question is, "No, not really." You see, no matter how hard we try, we cannot get right with God simply because we feel like we should be able to do that. It is that old human weakness of believing that ultimately we are in control of our own destiny.

A short look into biblical history is appropriate here. When the book of Titus was written, there was a considerable group of people who believed that only two things were eternal. This group, commonly known as the gnostics, believed that God and matter were eternal. The first of those things, God, was a good thing. The second, that of the material world, was not good. The gnostics believed that God created the world as we know it in stages that made sure God did not come in contact with what had been created. In this way, God would never have to be corrupted through contact with evil matter, like us! They believed that the only way for humankind to get right with God was to *think* their way back to God.

The truth for the gnostic was found in exercising their intellectual ability to its fullest. In this world, the smart people ruled, while the people the world deemed intellectual midgets were lost. So, the long and short of it was that the occupants of planet earth, if they ever hoped to find themselves in a right relationship with God, had to think their way through all of the interference, back to the Creator. In this world, the people with all the answers got to be with God, the rest were doomed!

Paul looked at this and said, as we have seen in the quote from Titus, that there was a better way for humankind to be in God's presence. You will remember that in an earlier chapter it was said that hope means different things to different people. Often the way we use it ("I hope tomorrow will be a better day than today" or "I hope I get the job I applied for") implies a certain amount of uncertainty. But, Christian hope has an entirely different quality about it, for it is grounded on the promises of God. It is not grounded on anything we can do, it is not really in our control at all! In his writing, Paul divides time into two distinct parts. First, before time, God made the promise of eternal life. That is, it was part of God's eternal will that God's children would enjoy eternal life. On top of that, Paul wants us to understand that God's promises are not like ours, because God cannot lie!

Paul's argument reaches full force, however, with the shift in time that occurs in verse 3. Here, Paul says that God manifested God's word at the proper time, and that God links this manifestation by the proclamation of God's word. Where is the hope in these verses? It is in the fact that Paul points out that God demonstrated the certainty of God's promises (God's word) in sending Jesus who died and was resurrected. Paul does not mention this explicitly here, but the thought is implicit.

Paul's focus in this passage from Titus is directed on God's plan to allow us to enter into eternal life. Now we see that God not only verified the truthfulness of God's promise, the certainty of hope, in sending Jesus into the world, but that God continues to do so through the proclamation of that word to the world.

We see once again that our Christian hope is built on the promise of God, not on any promise we may make. The promise is good because God does not lie and because God sent Jesus to keep that promise and make that promise available to everyone, not just those who think they can reason their way into God's graces.

Justification by grace says that we do not have the wisdom or energy to restore our relationship with God. But Jesus does. And when God allowed the "Word to become flesh and dwell among us," it was as if God was pushing the send button on an e-message to us all. Pushing that button began the process by which every human being is made right with God. You become the recipient of God's good grace, not because you sent a message to God, but because God has sent the message to you! You, in effect, become an heir in hope.

When you think about it, does someone who inherits something do anything to deserve the inheritance? Probably not. Inheritance is not a matter of *what* you are, it is, in all probability, more about *who* you are. And in this case, who are you? You are a child of God. You are justified, simply because God acted in Christ. That is a hope-filled idea, is it not?

Consequently, Christians can boldly live the kind of life prescribed in the Bible because God has intervened in human history to bring about a change. The whole idea of salvation, of rebirth and renewal, justification and hope, is reality, grounded in the historical events of Christ's ministry and death and resurrection. But to experience the new reality, the Christian must actively decide to step forward; the reality of the Christian possibility is not experienced through reciting a creed, but by living and performing it in faith. Therein lies hope, and therein lies the reason for our being justified by grace. A free gift, given freely to all, without any effort on our part. That is hope personified, it is a grace-filled life.

Questions For Your Consideration

1. How was Jesus' hopeless situation on Calvary turned into a hopeful situation for us?

2. What was the apostle Paul's concern when he wrote Titus? How do those concerns mirror our lives today?

3. Is it helpful or not to understand that in and of our own initiative we cannot bring God into our lives?

4. Describe why you think Martin Luther found the idea of "justification by grace" to be such an important part of the reformation.

5. Why is the idea presented throughout scripture that God cannot lie? Of what value is this notion?

6. Name some of the common threads that seem to run throughout the writing of the apostle Paul.

7. Although we are justified by grace, what promises do you think are important that we make to God? Why?

8. How do you show forth hope as you receive the gift of Jesus into your life?

9. Is it possible to be a hope-filled Christian without first incorporating all of the ideas presented thus far?

10. Give an example of how you live out the hope of Christ in your life.

Chapter Nine

Living Between Now And Not Yet

> *Even in his own land and among his own people, he was not accepted. But to all who believed him and accepted him, he gave the right to become children of God. They are reborn! This is not a physical birth resulting from human passion or plan — this rebirth comes from God.* — John 1:11-13

I am a child of God because I receive the free gift of grace that is offered to me through Jesus Christ, my Savior. I am a child of God because I receive the gift of eternal life through Jesus Christ, my Savior. When we are filled with that knowledge we know who we are now — today — we are children of God. This is not something that is going to happen to me sometime in the future, this is a present reality. Today I am a child of God.

Within some religious traditions, it is common to hear one person ask another, "If you died today, do you know that you would go to heaven?" An answer that often comes is, "I hope so. I've tried to live a good life and I would hope that God would receive me." That is a very different answer than John would have given. John knew he belonged to the Lord. He didn't have to wait until he died to find that out and neither should we.

Having said that, it is also true that how we live our lives should reflect the fact that we feel as if we are indeed children of God. We are hope-filled in all ways because we know that God knows who we are. Knowing that helps us to live a hope-filled life. It does not mean, however, that we live perfect lives, just lives that show forth a sense of now and not yet.

Robert Grudin, in *Time and the Art of Living*, does a masterful job of clarifying the point being made here.

> *Fast drivers can see no further than slow drivers, but they must look further down the road to time their reactions safely. Similarly, people with great projects afoot*

habitually look further and more clearly into the future than people who are mired in day-to-day concerns. These former control the future because by necessity they must project themselves into it; and the upshot is that, like ambitious settlers, they stake out larger plots and homesteads of time than the rest of us. They do not easily grow sad or old; they are seldom intimidated by the alarms and confusions of the present because they have something greater of their own, some sense of their large and coherent motion in time, to compare with the present.[1]

There is a kind of natural quality in hope-filled living that shows itself in a sense of gratitude for our good fortune at being children of God. There is a genuine sense of thankfulness that may be expressed in a variety of ways in our day-to-day activities. It represents the welling up of that open acknowledgment of good that demands expression in a word or act of thanksgiving. Such thanksgiving presupposes the kind of faith that is rooted in the firm conviction that God is working out everything in his purpose, and that there is genuine meaning beneath and beyond what meets the eye.

Living this kind of hope-filled life means that you can come to God for help whatever the need may be, even when you have failed and come short of what you think should have been accomplished. People of hope always seem to have great projects percolating in their minds. They have a boundless confidence in the things they are planning. They discover the very best in themselves and through themselves they are able to discover the best in others. They seem to know where they are going, because they know their ultimate destination! It is the difference between personal wholeness and the alternate feeling of never quite being sure of what or where you are going.

In our world today, we are faced with the troubling reality of terrorism. It is difficult to remember a time when people were more on edge in their day-to-day routines. There is a war between outward security and inward stability. There has probably never been a more poignant moment in time in terms of testing our hope-filled lives. As hope-filled children of God, there is always God's word to help us find strength and clarity in our walk of faith. We must always remember that the church leaders, who developed the faith that we cling to, experienced terrible moments of doubt and despair. Once again we turn to the apostle Paul for help.

> *And we know that God causes everything to work together for the good of those who love God and are called according to his purpose for them. For God knew his people in advance, and he chose them to become like his Son, so that his Son would be the firstborn, with many brothers and sisters. And having chosen them, he called them to come to him. And he gave them right standing with himself, and he promised them his glory.*
>
> *What can we say about such wonderful things as these? If God is for us, who can ever be against us?*
>
> — Romans 8:28-31

It is there that we see Paul knew about the now and the not yet. He knew how to equalize the living of life. There will always be tension, but the hope-filled Christian will balance that tension in healthy, not destructive ways. He knew that there would be times in our lives when we would need to find hope in the midst of terrorism. But, again notice that for Paul there is always a new possibility. There is always a larger picture for Paul. "If God is for us, who can ever be against us?" (v. 31). Life is more than those things that rob us of that hope we have found as children of God. Paul helps us to see that hope by giving us a look into the "not yet."

As children of God, we can focus our attention on Jesus, and when we do, we get outside of ourselves, we remove ourselves somewhat if only for a moment, from the distractions of the world. It is in these moments that we will be able to gain much-needed freedom in the way we see ourselves and the world around us. Knowing that we will always be children of God gives us hope in the present, while at the same time giving us a peek at the not yet. Hope allows us to be ever-changing, ever-aware, of our unique place in the cosmos.

Hope gives us an unchanging center in our lives. We all know that things around us change with or without our permission. That does not mean that we must change, as well. Hope reminds us that we have a purpose in living. We are not simply here to fill space and time. We are here to be the servants of the one who came to serve. It is not a hope based on silly expectations. Rather, it is hope based on a timeless promise from the one who created us. We have the assurance that even those things we do not understand, God understands. Jesus has showed us hope-filled possibilities.

> *But don't be afraid of those who threaten you. For the time is coming when everything will be revealed; all that is secret will be made public. What I tell you now in the darkness, shout abroad when daybreak comes. What I whisper in your ears, shout from the housetops for all to hear!*
>
> *Don't be afraid of those who want to kill you. They can only kill your body; they cannot touch your soul. Fear only God, who can destroy both soul and body in hell. Not even a sparrow, worth only half a penny, can fall to the ground without your Father knowing it. And the very hairs on your head are all numbered.*
>
> — Matthew 10:26-30

In some respects, what is being said is that although none of us gets through life without some trauma, all of us can be assured that the person who chooses hope can face whatever the problem is, knowing that they do not face it alone. That, in and of itself, is a pretty wonderful promise. In chapter 4 of Paul's letter to the Philippians, we read his hope-filled words.

> *Dear brothers and sisters, I love you and long to see you, for you are my joy and the reward for my work. So please stay true to the Lord, my dear friends.*
>
> *And now I want to plead with these two women, Euodia and Syntyche. Please, because you belong to the Lord, settle your disagreement. And I ask you, my true teammate, to help these women, for they worked hard with me in telling others the Good News. And they worked with Clement and the rest of my co-workers, whose names are written in the Book of Life.*

Always be full of joy in the Lord. I say it again — rejoice! Let everyone see that you are considerate in all you do. Remember, the Lord is coming soon.

Don't worry about anything; instead, pray about everything. Tell God what you need, and thank him for all he has given you. If you do this, you will experience God's peace, which is far more wonderful than the human mind can understand. His peace will guard your hearts and minds as you live in Christ Jesus.

— Philippians 4:1-7

True children of God, hope-filled and anxious to please God, know that true hopefulness comes when you learn to be grateful for the things that don't seem too good at the time. Paul pointed out that it is easy enough to be thankful for the good things, the hard part is the "not yet." But we can get through the now and into the not yet, because we do so with Christ as our leader and teacher. In the end, that is all we can hope for. It is all that we need.

---

1. Robert Grudin, *Time and the Art of Living* (San Francisco: Harper & Row, 1982), p. 6.

Questions For Your Consideration

1. Explain what John 1:13 means to you.

2. Talk about your idea of heaven. What is it — where is it — who gets to go?

3. How can a person who is ill look to the future with hope? Is it difficult for you to be hopeful with someone who is ill and tired of living?

4. How do you approach God when you need help? Give an example.

5. Has your sense of hope for the future been lowered since the terrorist attacks on our homeland?

6. What are the things that distract you enough to give the feeling that you are not a child of God?

7. Romans 8:28 says, "And we know that God causes everything to work together for the good of those who love God and are called according to the purpose for them." If this is true, then why do so many good people who love God find themselves in terrible situations in life?

8. Explain how hope can help you face those things in life that often seem insurmountable.

9. How can you be grateful for things you do not want in your life?

10. What is the "not yet" in your life?

Chapter Ten

Preserving The Hope-Filled Life

For I can do everything with the hope of Christ who gives me the strength I need. — Philippians 4:13

The book of Acts, which takes Paul's life right up to the end, does not record his final death after his arrival at Rome for the last time, but legends and traditions abound. Early tradition says that Paul died a martyr's death in Rome in the gladiator's ring and that he was resolute and unafraid to the end.

There, about 67 AD, he was imprisoned with Peter in the Mamertine prison, near the Roman Forum. Here, criminals and captives awaited execution or death in the gladiator's ring. In the second century, Tertullian of Carthage says Paul was beheaded. Gaius of Rome wrote in the third century that Paul suffered martyrdom on the Ostian Way. The third-century Christian theologian, Origen, recorded that Paul suffered martyrdom under Nero. The fourth-century Christian historian Eusebius made a similar statement.

Near the Ostian Way in Rome stands the magnificent basilica of St. Paul-Without-the-Walls, a monument to the fact that Paul was buried in this area.

Whatever the period and manner of his death, the voice of Paul rings out from 2 Timothy 4:7, "I have fought the good fight, I have finished the race, I have kept the faith." His is the voice of hope, even in the most desperate of situations. Paul lived and died as a man who understood that the resurrection was God's ultimate sign of hope to a troubled world.

The central event in the life of the Christian is the resurrection. Paul's word in Philippians and Timothy, as stated above, speaks to the fact that he has no doubt as to the power of the resurrection. It is at this point that the Christian community separates itself from all other world religions. That Jesus lived, that he died, and that he rose from the grave is the moment in history where hope finds its eternal dwelling. The resurrection is the historic reminder that God breaks the rules of what we may think possible. God says that all of our preconceived ideas mean nothing when it comes to the larger plan that God has for the world. We are not endowed with the ability to understand what those plans may be, but we are allowed a glimpse of that wonder when we enter into the reality of Easter. The resurrection is the ultimate reminder that God enters into the world when and where God chooses. Our hope is based on this one act. It is upon this event that all hope is based.

In his explanation of death and resurrection, Paul saw beyond his lifetime into the eternal, where he and other great souls are conformed to the body of Christ's glory. Following is Paul's explanation of the resurrection and its importance to those who would call themselves Christian.

Paul analyzes the resurrection, its assurance and logic, a fact that gave birth to the church we call Christian. Paul maintains confidence in the incredible mystery of Christ's resurrection. Paul declares, "And if we have hope in Christ only for this life, we are the most miserable people in the world" (1 Corinthians 15:19). Paul first repeats the historical evidence of the resurrection.

> *Let me remind you, dear brothers and sisters, of the Good News I preach to you before. You welcomed it then and still do now, for your faith is built on this wonderful message. And it is this Good News that saves you if you firmly believe it — unless, of course, you believed something that was never true in the first place.*
>
> *I passed on to you what was most important and what had also been passed on to me — that Christ died for our sins, just as the Scriptures said. He was buried, and he was raised from the dead on the third day, as the Scriptures said. He was seen by Peter and then by the twelve apostles. After that, he was seen by more than five hundred of his followers at one time, most of whom are still alive, though some have died by now. Then he was seen by James and later by all the apostles. Last of all, I saw him, too, long after the others, as though I had been born at the wrong time. For I am the*

least of all the apostles, and I am not worthy to be called an apostle after the way I persecuted the church of God.

But whatever I am now, it is all because God poured out his special favor on me — and not without results. For I have worked harder than all the other apostles, yet it was not I but God who was working through me by his grace. So it makes no difference whether I preach or they preach. The important thing is that you believed what we preached to you. — 1 Corinthians 15:1-11

He then goes on to explain that the denial of the resurrection signifies a denial of Christ's resurrection.

But tell me this — since we preach that Christ rose from the dead, why are some of you saying there will be no resurrection of the dead? For if there is no resurrection of the dead, then Christ has not been raised either. And if Christ was not raised, then all our preaching is useless, and your trust in God is useless. And we apostles would all be lying about God, for we have said that God raised Christ from the grave, but that can't be true if there is no resurrection of the dead. If there is no resurrection of the dead, then Christ has not been raised. And if Christ has not been raised, then your faith is useless, and you are still under condemnation for your sins. In that case, all who have died believing in Christ have perished! And if we have hope in Christ only for this life, we are the most miserable people in the world.
— 1 Corinthians 15:12-19

He eloquently explains the consequences of Christ's resurrection. But the fact is that Christ has been raised from the dead. He has become the first of a great harvest of those who will be raised to life again.

So you see, just as death came into the world through a man, Adam, now the resurrection from the dead has begun through another man, Christ. Everyone dies because all of us are related to Adam, the first man. But all who are related to Christ, the other man, will be given new life. But there is an order to this resurrection: Christ was raised first; then when Christ comes back, all his people will be raised.

After that the end will come, when he will turn the Kingdom over to God the Father, having put down all enemies of every kind. For Christ must reign until he humbles all his enemies beneath his feet. And the last enemy to be destroyed is death. For the Scriptures say, "God has given him authority over all things." (Of course, when it says "authority over all things," it does not include God himself, who gave Christ his authority.) Then, when he has conquered all things, the Son will present himself to God, so that God, who gave his Son authority over all things, will be utterly supreme over everything everywhere.

— 1 Corinthians 15:20-28

And finally he concludes this section.

If the dead will not be raised, then what point is there in people being baptized for those who are dead? Why do it unless the dead will someday rise again?

And why should we ourselves be continually risking our lives, facing death hour by hour? For I swear, dear brothers and sisters, I face death daily. This is as certain as my pride in what the Lord Jesus Christ has done in you. And what value was there in fighting wild beasts — those men of Ephesus — if there will be no resurrection from the dead? If there is no resurrection, "Let's feast and get drunk, for tomorrow we die!"

Don't be fooled by those who say such things, for "bad company corrupts good character." Come to your senses and stop sinning. For to your shame I say that some of you don't even know God.

— 1 Corinthians 15:29-34

Do you see the hope? He says that he faces death every single day and still he moves forward, often without any regard for his own personal safety. Paul is the example we all should look to when it comes to being a hopeful people. And he is clear to all that it is at the point of our earthly body's death that the resurrection moment becomes most mysterious and most understood (1 Corinthians 15:36).

What a foolish question! When you put a seed into the ground, it doesn't grow into a plant unless it dies first (1 Corinthians 15:36). So it is with the body laid in the grave. In the same manner, a heavenly body arises into another dimension we cannot see and is ready for a new mode of existence and a new set of relationships we cannot even comprehend.

Like the sun, moon, and stars born out of the darkness, but finally evolving into varying degrees of color and hue, so will humankind's resurrected body be. That is to say we may not understand the mystery that is resurrection, but like the universe around us, we dare not deny it! Paul's hope-filled life and message is one that says Christ's resurrected body was so wondrous that we cannot even begin to comprehend the wonder of it. A perfect abode for the spirit and free from the limitations and imperfections of the material body, it could even pass through closed doors and finally even return to the right hand of the one who created him.

Hope is a many-sided emotion and it comes to us in many and varied forms. Just so, with the resurrected life that Paul lived and died to communicate to us.

> *But let me tell you a wonderful secret God has revealed to us. Not all of us will die, but we will all be transformed ... For our perishable earthly bodies must be transformed into heavenly bodies that will never die.*
>
> *When this happens — when our perishable earthly bodies have been transformed into heavenly bodies that will never die — then at last the Scriptures will come true: "Death is swallowed up in victory. O death, where is your victory? O death, where is your sting?"*
>
> — 1 Corinthians 15:51, 53-55

As one becomes a new creation in God, one's fear of death begins to recede into the background of life. It is not that a Christian does not fear the unknown, it is rather that the unknown is not some scary place that we need fear. It is a place where Jesus has already been and where Jesus will greet us again. Talk about hope!

Paul's triumphant explanation of the resurrection helps us to know that there is quite literally no place on earth or in heaven that we are left helpless. The kind of hope Paul lived with rose above every material affliction: chains, imprisonment, beatings, hunger, illness, and finally even death itself.

He, whose life had been radiant with hope, he who knew the true meaning of the resurrection, he who had lifted so many out of despair, could not be hopeless even as he himself followed his Lord into eternity. His is a message that transcends our foolish pride, our arrogance, our disbelief, even our death. And from a prison cell in Rome, he sends this final hopeful message in this study.

> *So I pray that God, who gives you hope, will keep you happy and full of peace as you believe in him. May you overflow with hope through the power of the Holy Spirit.*
> — Romans 15:13

Amen.

Questions For Your Consideration

1. What can you do with Jesus as your Savior that you could not do without him?

2. Does it matter to you how Paul died? Why or why not?

3. When someone dies, are they really dead? If you answer, "Yes," then explain how someone who has died can live again.

4. Other than the resurrection, how does God break the rules as we know them? For example, can a young woman have a baby without having sex?

5. Why was it that Paul was imprisoned in Rome and not put to death by crucifixion as others who were considered criminals?

6. Are you bothered by the fact that you cannot explain, in any rational human way, how Jesus was raised from the grave?

7. Where is the hope in the readings in this chapter? Go back as a group and count the times that the word "hope" or an idea that is hopeful is present.

8. Are any of the hopeful things you defined from question 7 relevant to your life today?

9. How do the words of Paul in 1 Corinthians 15 help, or conversely confuse you when it comes to better understanding the resurrection?

10. Give an example of what hope means to you and how you have changed that idea during the course of this study. Share your answers aloud with each other.

Resource Material

Alves, Ruben Azevedo. *Theology of Human Hope*. Corpus Books, Washington DC, 1969.

Bornkamm, Gunther. *Paul*, tr. by D. M. G. Stalker. Harper & Row, New York, 1971.

Braaten, Carl E. *The Future of God: The Revolutionary Dynamics of Hope*. Harper & Row, New York, 1969.

Fackre, Gabriel J. *The Rainbow Sign*, paperback. Eerdmans, Grand Rapids, Michigan, 1969.

Fosdick, Harry Emerson. *The Hope of the World*. Country Life Press, Garden City, New York, 1953.

Gibran, Kahlil. *A Tear and a Smile*. Alfred A. Knopf, New York, 1950.

Kraeling, Emil G. *I Have Kept the Faith: The Life of the Apostle Paul*. Rand McNally, Chicago, 1965.

Lynch, William R. *Images of Hope*, paperback. Metro-Omega books, New American Library, New York, 1965.

Marty, Martin E., and Dean G. Peerman, eds. *New Theology No. 5*. Macmillan, Toronto, New York, London, 1969.

Moltmann, Jurgen. *Theology of Hope*, tr. by James W. Leitch. Harper & Row, New York, 1965.

Pollock, John. *The Apostle: A Life of Paul*. Doubleday, Garden City, New York, 1969.

Sherman, Franklin E., ed. *Christian Hope and the Future of Humanity*, paperback. Augsburg, Minneapolis, 1970.

Woodyard, David. *Beyond Cynicism: The Practice of Hope*. Westminster Press, Philadelphia, 1952.

Zimmerli, Walter. *Man and His Hope in the New Testament*. Alex R. Allenson, Naperville, Illinois, 1971.

www.ingramcontent.com/pod-product-compliance
Lightning Source LLC
LaVergne TN
LVHW020652100826
845148LV00012B/2450